C000296375

ONE BIG FAMILY

Twenty new songs for contemporary all-age worship

by

WILLIAM LLEWELLYN & TIMOTHY DUDLEY-SMITH

RS♦M

Published in the UK in 2018 by
THE ROYAL SCHOOL OF CHURCH MUSIC
19 The Close, Salisbury, Wilts, SP1 2EB

Tel: +44 (0)1722 424848
Email: press@rscm.com Website: www.rscm.org.uk

Registered charity 312828

ONE BIG FAMILY

Compilation © 2018 by Timothy Dudley-Smith and William Llewellyn

Permission to reproduce music: Though the music is copyright and may not be copied or reproduced
in any form without the permission of the author or publishers, holders of a CCLI (Christian Copyright
Licensing International) Music Reproduction Licence may reproduce any of these songs within the terms
of their licence, noting the use on their CCLI return in the usual way. Requests to reproduce music where
permission is not given by an appropriate CCLI licence should be addressed to the Music Rights and
Contracts Manager, Oxford University Press, Great Clarendon Street, Oxford, OX2 6DP, UK

Permission to reproduce texts: Though these texts are copyright and may not be copied or reproduced in
any form without the permission of the author or publishers, holders of a CCLI (Christian Copyright
Licensing International) licence may reproduce any of these texts within the terms of their licence,
noting the use on their CCLI return in the usual way. Requests within Europe and Africa to reproduce words
where permission is not given by an appropriate CCLI licence should be addressed to the Music Rights
and Contracts Manager, Oxford University Press, Great Clarendon Street, Oxford, OX2 6DP, UK
and from the rest of the world to Hope Publishing Company, 380 South Main Place, Carol Stream, Illinois, IL 60188, USA.
Website: www.hopepublishing.com
email: hope@hopepublishing.com

Timothy Dudley-Smith has asserted his moral rights to be identified as
the author of this work under the Copyright, Designs and Patents Act, 1988.

William Llewellyn has asserted his moral rights to be identified as
the composer of this work under the Copyright, Designs and Patents Act, 1988.

ISBN: 978-0-85402-273-1

Also by the same author and music editor:

Beneath a Travelling Star: forty-five contemporary hymns and carols for Christmas
A Calendar of Praise: thirty contemporary hymns for seasons of the Christian Year
High Days and Holy Days: thirty contemporary hymns for annual occasions
in the life of the local church
The Voice of Faith: thirty contemporary hymns for Saints' Days
or based on the liturgy
Above Every Name: thirty contemporary hymns in praise of Christ
Draw Near to God: thirty contemporary hymns for worship, mainly for the pastoral Services
A Mirror to the Soul: thirty contemporary hymns based on the psalms

Cover design by Anthony Marks
Music Engraving by William Llewellyn, Devon, UK
Audio CD arranged and produced by Anthony Marks
Typesetting and layout by RSCM PRESS
Printed in England by Halstan & Co, Amersham

CONTENTS

Preface   6

***

GOD THE FATHER

1. **God the Creator of all**
   'Our God made the planets to circle in space'   GOD'S CREATION   8 / 49
   see also No.16, 'This wonderful world we live in'

2. **God who loves us**
   'God is Love, God is Love!'   KIND AND LOVING   10 / 50
   see also No.12, 'For the world that we live in'

THE LORD JESUS CHRIST

see also THE CHRISTIAN YEAR

3. **Jesus, his person, life & ministry**
   'The Bible tells of Jesus' birth'   THE BIBLE TELLS   12 / 51

4. **Jesus, our example**
   'Give thanks to Jesus'   GIVE THANKS   14 / 52

5. **Jesus, our teacher**
   'Jesus taught us to be kind and loving'   JESUS TAUGHT US   16 / 53

6. **Jesus, King of glory**
   'Jesus our King'   SING TO THE KING   18 / 54

THE HOLY SPIRIT

7. **His presence and fruit**
   'Spirit of God, be here among us'   SPIRIT AMONG US   20 / 55

THE CHRISTIAN YEAR

8. **Jesus, his birth: Christmas**
   'So still, so still!'   SO STILL   22 / 56

9. **Jesus in the desert: Lent**
   'When Jesus Christ was all alone'   CHRIST TEMPTED   24 / 57

10. **Jesus in Jerusalem: Palm Sunday**
   'Jesus was riding on a donkey'   HOSANNA TO THE KING   26 / 58

11. **Jesus, his cross: Passiontide**
   'Jesus, once you suffered for me'   JESUS SET ME FREE   28 / 59

12. **Jesus risen from the dead: Eastertide**
   'Jesus risen! The stone rolled away'   JESUS RISEN   30 / 60

13. **Jesus ascended into heaven: Ascensiontide**
   'I am with you always'   LOVE ALWAYS   32 / 61

   The Holy Spirit: Pentecost
   see No. 7: 'Spirit of God, be here among us'

THE CHRISTIAN LIFE

14. **Thankfulness**
   'For the world that we live in'   PRAISE FOR THE WORLD   34 / 62
   see also No.4: 'Give thanks to Jesus'

15. **Prayer**
   'Lord, we want to learn to pray'   PRAISE AND PRAY   36 / 63

16. **The Bible**
   'The Bible is a shining light'   SHINING LIGHT   38 / 64
   see also Nos. 3: 'The Bible tells of Jesus' birth'
   & 15: 'Lord, we want to learn to pray'

17. **The Fight of Faith**
   'We are soldiers of the King'   MARCH AND SING   40 / 65

18. **Sharing the Good News**
   'Tell the world'   TELL THE WORLD   42 / 66

19. **Care for Creation**
   'This wonderful world we live in'   CARE FOR THE WORLD   44 / 67
   see also No.1: 'Our God made
   the planets to circle in space'

20. **The Family of the Church**
      ONE BIG FAMILY   46 / 68

* * *

INDEX OF TUNES

by William Llewellyn

* * *

CARE FOR THE WORLD	19
CHRIST TEMPTED	9
GIVE THANKS	4
GOD'S CREATION	1
HOSANNA TO THE KING	10
JESUS RISEN	12
JESUS SET ME FREE	11
JESUS TAUGHT US	5
KIND AND LOVING	2
LOVE ALWAYS	13
MARCH AND SING	17
ONE BIG FAMILY	20
PRAISE AND PRAY	15
PRAISE FOR THE WORLD	14
SHINING LIGHT	16
SING TO THE KING	6
SO STILL	8
SPIRIT AMONG US	7
TELL THE WORLD	18
THE BIBLE TELLS	3

PREFACE

THE YOUNGER MEMBERS of a Christian fellowship are sometimes called 'the church of tomorrow': but in fact they are part of the church of today, just as much as their mums and dads, or the grey heads in any congregation. It seems clear from the Gospels that children had a special place in the affections of the Lord Jesus Christ on earth. In Matthew 18 & 19, for example, we find his words about the need (as AV translates it) 'to be converted and become as little children', about how anyone who welcomes a child in Jesus' name 'is welcoming me', and about how 'you must let the little children come to me and never stop them. The kingdom of Heaven belongs to little children like these' (so J.B.Phillips).

These twenty hymns or songs represent our attempt to offer those who lead children in Family Worship, whether at home, school or church, a few additions to what they might sing. The current experiments in 'Fresh Expressions' or 'Messy Church' would be one obvious example. Although the Contents page shows some arrangement of these songs, there are inevitably vast gaps. In the Christian Year, for instance, we have nothing on Advent or Epiphany; nor on Jesus' baptism, stories or miracles. We have simply done what, at least for the moment, we feel we can.

So what characteristics have we sought? First, memorable and indeed catchy tunes, easily learned and happily sung. Next, a content never far from the teaching of the Bible, and related to the walk of faith as a child may understand it. We have aimed for simplicity, with plenty of repetition, and an appeal to the young imagination. Above all, as can be seen from the Contents page, Jesus himself is our central theme. In her book about children, *Half Angels,* (London, 1961) Elisabeth Montefiore asks herself, 'What do we want them to learn?', and answers, 'First and always to love Jesus Christ'. That must be our touchstone; there is surely nothing better anyone can offer a child.

Of course the teaching content is bound to be very limited. But we see the singing as an adjunct to stories and teaching, not a substitute for them. Indeed, it is only in some understanding of their context that most of these songs can be sung with meaning. As will be clear from even a glance at what follows, we have written for a variety of ages and not every hymn or song will be suitable for any given group of children. But we believe there is nothing here that an adult will be embarrassed to sing in the company of children, or that a child will have to 'unlearn' in later years.

In 1848 Miss Cecil Humphreys ('Fanny' to the family), just turning thirty, published her *Hymns for Little Children*; she was to become much better known over the years by her married name as Mrs Alexander. Her collection, touchingly dedicated to her young godsons, sought to help them know and understand the teachings of their church (in her case, the Church of Ireland), especially the Commandments and the Creed. Today, of her forty texts, most have well outlived their usefulness and are sunk without trace. But three especially remain in common use, and are still to be found in many twenty-first century hymnals. They are 'All things bright and beautiful', written about God as Creator; 'Once in royal David's city' on the Incarnation; and 'There is a green hill far away' about the sufferings and Cross of Christ.

Our work does not aspire to such longevity! But if one of these hymns or songs serves to lift the worship of younger voices, and perhaps to be of use, under God's hand, to inform a child's understanding and to help towards a love for the Lord Jesus Christ, who could ask for more?

William Llewellyn
Timothy Dudley-Smith

Colyton, Devon
Ford, Salisbury

September 2017

BACKING TRACKS

The CD enclosed with this book provides backing tracks for all the songs in *One Big Family*. Each song has a brief introduction, which is repeated between verses. Songs which have only one verse are played through twice.

LEAD SHEETS

At the back of the book, we have provided lead sheets that include the melody line, lyrics and guitar chords. All chords are provided at pitch. If your church has a CCLI Music Reproduction Licence, these pages may be photocopied for church use. Please report usage of these songs in your annual reporting to CCLI.

1 Our God made the planets

GOD'S CREATION

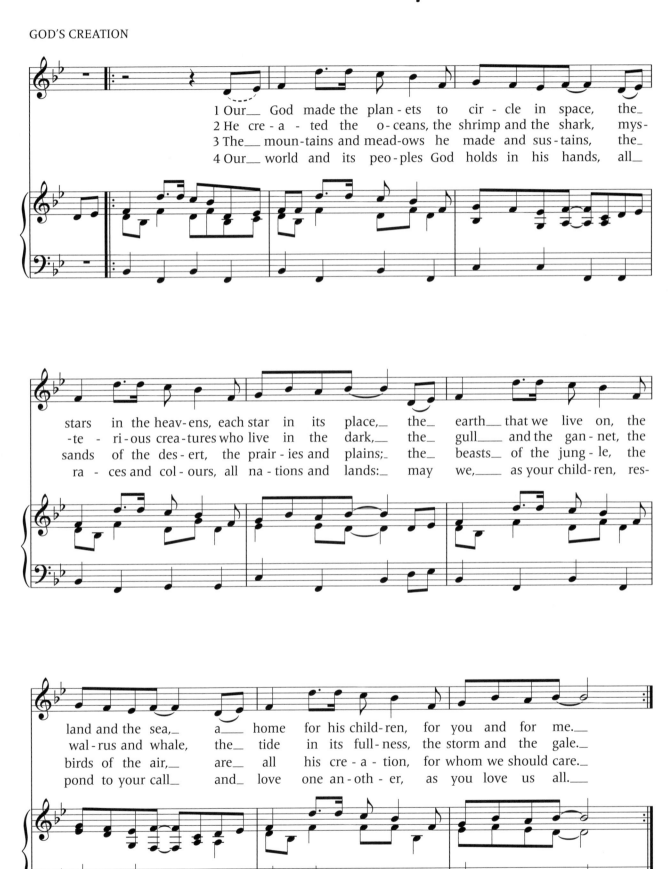

1 Our__ God made the plan-ets to cir-cle in space, the__
2 He cre-a-ted the o-ceans, the shrimp and the shark, mys-
3 The__ moun-tains and mead-ows he made and sus-tains, the__
4 Our__ world and its peo-ples God holds in his hands, all__

stars in the heav-ens, each star in its place,__ the__ earth__ that we live on, the
-te-ri-ous crea-tures who live in the dark,__ the__ gull__ and the gan-net, the
sands of the des-ert, the prair-ies and plains;__ the__ beasts__ of the jung-le, the
ra-ces and col-ours, all na-tions and lands:__ may we,__ as your child-ren, res-

land and the sea,__ a__ home for his child-ren, for you and for me.__
wal-rus and whale, the__ tide in its full-ness, the storm and the gale.__
birds of the air,__ are__ all his cre-a-tion, for whom we should care.__
pond to your call__ and__ love one an-oth-er, as you love us all.__

OUR GOD MADE THE PLANETS to circle in space,
the stars in the heavens, each star in its place,
the earth that we live on, the land and the sea,
a home for his children, for you and for me.

2 He created the oceans, the shrimp and the shark,
mysterious creatures who live in the dark,
the gull and the gannet, the walrus and whale,
the tide in its fullness, the storm and the gale.

3 The mountains and meadows he made and sustains,
the sands of the desert, the prairies and plains;
the beasts of the jungle, the birds of the air,
are all his creation, for whom we should care.

4 Our world and its peoples God holds in his hands,
all races and colours, all nations and lands:
may we, as your children, respond to your call
and love one another, as you love us all.

Words: Timothy Dudley-Smith © administered by Oxford University Press in Europe (including UK and Ireland) and
Africa, and by Hope Publishing Company in all other territories (including USA)
Music: William Llewellyn © 2017 Oxford University Press, Great Clarendon Street, Oxford OX2 6DP

2 God is Love, God is Love!

KIND AND LOVING

God is Love, God is Love! Kind and lov-ing is
he; God is Love, God is Love! He is lov-ing to me.
He it is who hears our prayers from his home a - bove,
and in Je - sus loves and cares, God is Love!

GOD IS LOVE, God is Love!
Kind and loving is he;
God is Love, God is Love!
He is loving to me.
He it is who hears our prayers
from his home above,
and in Jesus loves and cares,
God is Love!

Words: Timothy Dudley-Smith © administered by Oxford University Press in Europe (including UK and Ireland) and
Africa, and by Hope Publishing Company in all other territories (including USA)
Music: William Llewellyn © 2017 Oxford University Press, Great Clarendon Street, Oxford OX2 6DP

3 The Bible tells of Jesus' birth

THE BIBLE TELLS

1. The Bi-ble tells of Je-sus' birth, Je-sus' birth, Je-sus' birth, the
2. The Bi-ble tells what Je-sus said, Je-sus said, Je-sus said, who
3. The Bi-ble tells how Je-sus died, Je-sus died, Je-sus died, the
4. The Bi-ble tells how Je-sus lives, Je-sus lives, Je-sus lives, and

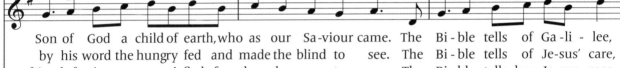

Son of God a child of earth, who as our Sa-viour came. The Bi-ble tells of Ga-li - lee,
by his word the hungry fed and made the blind to see. The Bi-ble tells of Je-sus' care,
friend of sin-ners, cru-ci-fied for those he came to save. The Bi-ble tells how Je-sus rose,
how a-bund-ant life he gives to those for whom he came. The Bi-ble shows him as our friend,

Ga - li - lee, Ga - li - lee, where Je - sus taught be - side the sea, and healed the sick and lame.
Je - sus' care, Je - sus' care, for all God's child-ren ev - ery where, in - clud-ing you and me.
Je - sus rose, Je - sus rose, no long-er now in death's re - pose but ris - en from the grave!
as our friend, as our friend, who walks be - side us to the end, and knows us all by name.

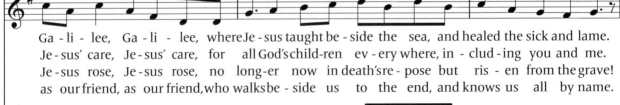

THE BIBLE tells of Jesus' birth,
　　Jesus' birth, Jesus' birth,
the Son of God a child of earth,
　　who as our Saviour came.
The Bible tells of Galilee,
　　Galilee, Galilee,
where Jesus taught beside the sea,
　　and healed the sick and lame.

2　The Bible tells what Jesus said,
　　Jesus said, Jesus said,
who by his word the hungry fed
　　and made the blind to see.
The Bible tells of Jesus' care,
　　Jesus' care, Jesus' care,
for all God's children everywhere,
　　including you and me.

3　The Bible tells how Jesus died,
　　Jesus died, Jesus died,
the friend of sinners, crucified
　　for those he came to save.
The Bible tells how Jesus rose,
　　Jesus rose, Jesus rose,
no longer now in death's repose
　　but risen from the grave!

4　The Bible tells how Jesus lives,
　　Jesus lives, Jesus lives,
and how abundant life he gives
　　to those for whom he came.
The Bible shows him as our friend,
　　as our friend, as our friend,
who walks beside us to the end,
　　and knows us all by name.

Words: Timothy Dudley-Smith © administered by Oxford University Press in Europe (including UK and Ireland) and
Africa, and by Hope Publishing Company in all other territories (including USA)
Music: William Llewellyn © 2017 Oxford University Press, Great Clarendon Street, Oxford OX2 6DP

14

4 Give thanks to Jesus

GIVE THANKS

1. Give thanks to Je-sus, give praise to his Name; born as our Sa-viour, from heav-en he came; li-ving a-mong us, our King and our Friend, love is his king-dom and life with-out end._ 2. With his Fa-ther he now reigns a-bove; in his king-dom

he is King of Love.   To us his child-ren he shows what to do:__

'Love   one   an - oth - er,   as   I   have loved   you.'__

G IVE THANKS to Jesus,
    give praise to his Name;
born as our Saviour,
    from heaven he came;
living among us,
    our King and our Friend,
love is his kingdom
    and life without end.

2 With his Father
    he now reigns above;
in his kingdom
    he is King of Love.
To us his children
    he shows what to do:
'Love one another,
    as I have loved you.'

Words: Timothy Dudley-Smith © administered by Oxford University Press in Europe (including UK and Ireland) and
Africa, and by Hope Publishing Company in all other territories (including USA)
Music: William Llewellyn © 2017 Oxford University Press, Great Clarendon Street, Oxford OX2 6DP

5 Jesus taught us to be kind and loving

JESUS TAUGHT US

Je - sus taught us to be kind and lov - ing, and to
Make and keep_ us ev-er strong and faith - ful,___

be his friends in all we say___ and do;___ Je - sus taught us to be
make and keep_ us ev - er loy - al and true,___ help us, Je - sus, to be

Fine

strong and faith - ful, Je - sus taught us to be loy - al and true.
kind and lov - ing and to be your friends in all we say___ and do.___

Je - sus, Mast- er, our Lord and our King, help us learn from this song that we sing.

JESUS TAUGHT US to be kind and loving,
and to be his friends in all we say and do;
Jesus taught us to be strong and faithful,
Jesus taught us to be loyal and true.

Jesus, Master, our Lord and our King,
help us learn from this song we sing.

2 Make and keep us ever strong and faithful,
make and keep us ever loyal and true,
help us, Jesus, to be kind and loving,
and to be your friends in all we say and do.

Words: Timothy Dudley-Smith © administered by Oxford University Press in Europe (including UK and Ireland) and
Africa, and by Hope Publishing Company in all other territories (including USA)
Music: William Llewellyn © 2017 Oxford University Press, Great Clarendon Street, Oxford OX2 6DP

6 Jesus our King

SING TO THE KING

Je-sus our King, Lord and Sa-viour! Je-sus our friend, with us now:_ joy-full-y sing, he is near us, and will hear us sing to the King!_

JESUS our King,
Lord and Saviour!
Jesus our friend,
with us now:
joyfully sing,
he is near us,
and will hear us
sing to the King!

Words: Timothy Dudley-Smith © administered by Oxford University Press in Europe (including UK and Ireland) and
Africa, and by Hope Publishing Company in all other territories (including USA)
Music: William Llewellyn © 2017 Oxford University Press, Great Clarendon Street, Oxford OX2 6DP

7 Spirit of God, be here among us

SPIRIT AMONG US

Spi-rit of God, be here a-mong us,
Spi-rit di-vine, be here a-mong us,

Spi-rit of God,_ be here a-mong us! Come from a-bove,
Spi-rit di-vine, be here a-mong us! Teach us to sing_

1.
Spi-rit of love,_ your love, joy and peace be here a-mong us!

2.
'Je-sus is King,' his Spi-rit of love_ be here a-mong us!

SPIRIT OF GOD, be here among us,
Spirit of God, be here among us!
Come from above,
Spirit of love,
your love, joy and peace be here among us!

2 Spirit divine, be here among us,
Spirit divine, be here among us!
Teach us to sing
'Jesus is King,'
his Spirit of love be here among us!

Words: Timothy Dudley-Smith © administered by Oxford University Press in Europe (including UK and Ireland) and
Africa, and by Hope Publishing Company in all other territories (including USA)
Music: William Llewellyn © 2017 Oxford University Press, Great Clarendon Street, Oxford OX2 6DP

8 So still, so still!

SO STILL

Rocking gently

1. So still,_____ so still!_____ the star‑light is frost‑y and chill; the flocks are a‑sleep while shep‑herds must keep their watch in the night on the hill:_____

2. Till dawn,_____ till dawn!_____ there breaks what a won‑der‑ful morn! With an‑gels we sing to wel‑come our King; King Je‑sus the Sa‑viour is born!_____

3. Sing praise,_____ sing praise!_____ a ca‑rol of thank‑ful‑ness raise! God gave in his love his Son from a‑bove at Christ‑mas, the day of all days,_____

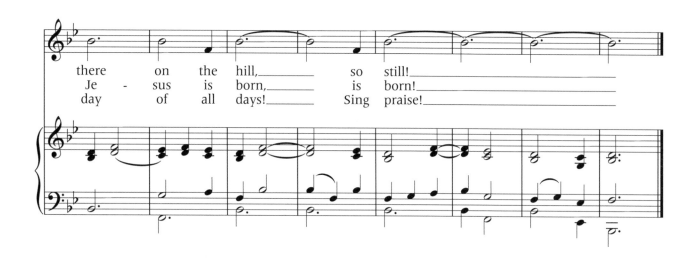

S O STILL, so still!
the starlight is frosty and chill;
the flocks are asleep
while shepherds must keep
their watch in the night on the hill:
there on the hill,
so still!

2 Till dawn, till dawn!
there breaks what a wonderful morn!
With angels we sing
to welcome our King;
King Jesus the Saviour is born!
Jesus is born,
is born!

3 Sing praise, sing praise!
a carol of thankfulness raise!
God gave in his love
his Son from above
at Christmas, the day of all days,
days of all days!
Sing praise!

Words: Timothy Dudley-Smith © administered by Oxford University Press in Europe (including UK and Ireland) and Africa, and by Hope Publishing Company in all other territories (including USA)
Music: William Llewellyn © 2017 Oxford University Press, Great Clarendon Street, Oxford OX2 6DP

9 When Jesus Christ was all alone

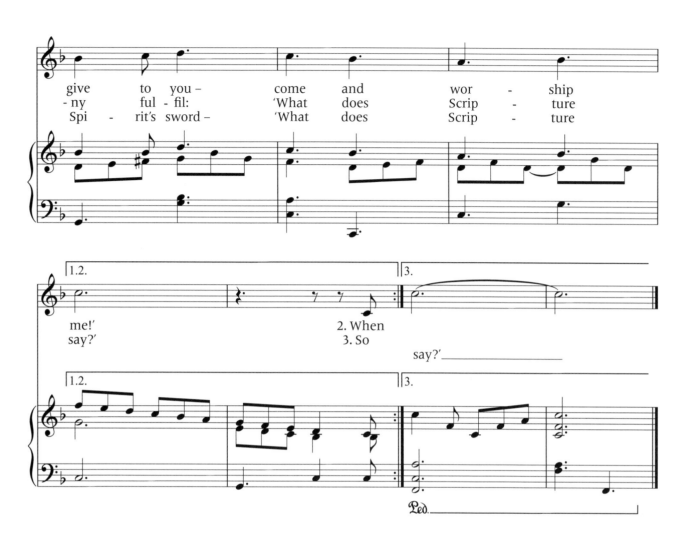

WHEN JESUS CHRIST was all alone
Satan came and said,
'I know you're hungry, here's a stone,
  make it turn to bread;
your mighty works of wonder do,
  everyone will see,
and all the world I'll give to you –
  come and worship me!'

2 When Satan came to tempt the Lord
  he was sent away,
for Jesus knew God's written word,
  'What does Scripture say?'
He chose to do his Father's will,
  his Father's word obey,
and so his destiny fulfil:
  'What does Scripture say?'

3 So now when tempted to do wrong
  we need never stray;
we look to Jesus and are strong:
  'What does Scripture say?'
The power of God is in his word,
  strength for every day,
our Bible is the Spirit's sword –
  'What does Scripture say?'

Words: Timothy Dudley-Smith © administered by Oxford University Press in Europe (including UK and Ireland) and Africa, and by Hope Publishing Company in all other territories (including USA)
Music: William Llewellyn © 2017 Oxford University Press, Great Clarendon Street, Oxford OX2 6DP

10 Jesus was riding on a donkey

HOSANNA TO THE KING

JESUS was riding on a donkey
when the people of Jerusalem
cried 'Hosanna to the Son of David,'
    and Hosanna we will sing with them!
        Hosanna,
        Hosanna,
Hosanna we will sing with them!

2 Jesus was teaching in the temple
    when the children of Jerusalem
cried 'Hosanna to the Son of David,'
    and Hosanna we will sing with them!
        Hosanna,
        Hosanna,
Hosanna we will sing with them!

3 Jesus is still the friend of children,
    let us listen and obey his word;
sing Hosanna to the King of Glory,
    and Hosanna to the risen Lord,
        Hosanna,
        Hosanna,
Hosanna to the risen Lord!

Words: Timothy Dudley-Smith © administered by Oxford University Press in Europe (including UK and Ireland) and Africa, and by Hope Publishing Company in all other territories (including USA)
Music: William Llewellyn © 2017 Oxford University Press, Great Clarendon Street, Oxford OX2 6DP

11 Jesus, once you suffered for me

JESUS SET ME FREE

1. Je - sus, once you suf-fered for me,
2. All my sins you car - ried for me,
3. Je - sus lives, a Sav-iour for me,

gave your life on Cal - va - ry's tree, great - er lov - ing there
hang - ing there on Cal - va - ry's tree, in your dy - ing you
emp - ty now is Cal - va - ry's tree, King of heav - en and

can - not be: thank you, dear Lord Je - sus!
set me free: thank you, dear Lord Je - sus!
earth is he: thank you, dear Lord Je - sus!

JESUS, once you suffered for me,
gave your life on Calvary's tree,
greater loving there cannot be:
    thank you, dear Lord Jesus!

2 All my sins you carried for me,
    hanging there on Calvary's tree,
    in your dying you set me free:
        thank you, dear Lord Jesus!

3 Jesus lives, a Saviour for me,
    empty now is Calvary's tree,
    King of heaven and earth is he:
        thank you, dear Lord Jesus!

Words: Timothy Dudley-Smith © administered by Oxford University Press in Europe (including UK and Ireland) and
Africa, and by Hope Publishing Company in all other territories (including USA)
Music: William Llewellyn © 2017 Oxford University Press, Great Clarendon Street, Oxford OX2 6DP

12 Jesus risen! The stone rolled away

JESUS RISEN

Je - sus ris - en! The stone rolled a - way!

Come and see where his poor bo - dy lay.___ Je - sus ris - en, in

glo - ry ris - en, a - live and ris - en, and with us to - day!___

JESUS risen!
The stone rolled away!
Come and see
where his poor body lay.
Jesus risen,
in glory risen,
alive and risen,
and with us today!

Words: Timothy Dudley-Smith © administered by Oxford University Press in Europe (including UK and Ireland) and
Africa, and by Hope Publishing Company in all other territories (including USA)
Music: William Llewellyn © 2017 Oxford University Press, Great Clarendon Street, Oxford OX2 6DP

13 I am with you always

LOVE ALWAYS

1. I am with you al-ways, al-ways, al-ways,
2. I am with you al-ways, al-ways, al-ways,
3. We would love you al-ways, al-ways, al-ways,

I am with you al-ways, Je-sus gave his word;
I am with you al-ways, if you are my friend;
we would love you al-ways, we will be your friends;

I am with you al-ways,
I am with you al-ways,
we would love you al-ways,

al-ways, al-ways, I am with you al-ways, Sav-iour, Friend and Lord.
al-ways, al-ways, I am with you al-ways, to the journ-ey's end.
al-ways, al-ways, we would love you al-ways till the journ-ey ends!

I am with you always,
always, always,
I am with you always,
    Jesus gave his word;
I am with you always,
    always, always,
I am with you always,
    Saviour, Friend and Lord.

2 I am with you always,
    always, always,
I am with you always
    if you are my friend;
I am with you always,
    always, always,
I am with you always
    to the journey's end.

3 We would love you always,
    always, always,
we would love you always,
    we will be your friends;
we would love you always,
    always, always,
we would love you always
    till the journey ends!

Words: Timothy Dudley-Smith © administered by Oxford University Press in Europe (including UK and Ireland) and Africa, and by Hope Publishing Company in all other territories (including USA)
Music: William Llewellyn © 2017 Oxford University Press, Great Clarendon Street, Oxford OX2 6DP

14 For the world that we live in

PRAISE FOR THE WORLD

For the world that we live_ in, let us praise to-day!_ for our food and our friends,_ and for our work and play._ For the life we are gi-ven let us join to sing,_ as we thank you, our Fa-ther God, for ev-ery-thing!__

FOR THE WORLD that we live in,
let us praise today!
for our food and our friends,
    and for our work and play.
For the life we are given
    let us join to sing,
 as we thank you, our Father God,
    for everything!

Words: Timothy Dudley-Smith © administered by Oxford University Press in Europe (including UK and Ireland) and
Africa, and by Hope Publishing Company in all other territories (including USA)
Music: William Llewellyn © 2017 Oxford University Press, Great Clarendon Street, Oxford OX2 6DP

15 Lord, we want to learn to pray

PRAISE AND PRAY

1. Lord, we want to learn to pray,
3. Teach us how to praise and pray,

read the Bi-ble day by day, un-der-stand, be-lieve, o-bey, Je-sus our Lord._
read the Bi-ble day by day, live our lives in Je-sus' way, Je-sus our Lord._

Fine

2. Lord, we want to learn to pray, help us mean the words we say,

live our lives in Je-sus' way, Je-sus our Lord._

Fa - ther God, at home in heaven, thank you for the

D.S. al Fine

life you've given; so we ask:

D.S. al Fine

LORD, we want to learn to pray,
read the Bible day by day,
understand, believe, obey,
　Jesus our Lord.

Lord, we want to learn to pray,
help us mean the words we say,
live our lives in Jesus' way,
　Jesus our Lord.

　　Father God, at home in heaven
　　thank you for the life you've given;
　　so we ask:

2　Teach us how to praise and pray,
　read the Bible day by day,
　live our lives in Jesus' way,
　　Jesus our Lord.

Words: Timothy Dudley-Smith © administered by Oxford University Press in Europe (including UK and Ireland) and Africa, and by Hope Publishing Company in all other territories (including USA)
Music: William Llewellyn © 2017 Oxford University Press, Great Clarendon Street, Oxford OX2 6DP

16 The Bible is a shining light

SHINING LIGHT

1. The Bible is a shining light, shining light, shining light, a lamp to lead us through the night and guide us on our way._____ The Bible is a book of truth, book of truth, book of truth, the

2. The Bible is our daily bread, daily bread, daily bread, the food by which our souls are fed to keep us true and strong._____ The Bible is the Spirit's sword, Spirit's sword, Spirit's sword, the

3. The Bible is the living seed, living seed, living seed, to grow within us, as we read, the life of God above._____ So open, Lord, my eyes to see, eyes to see, eyes to see, the

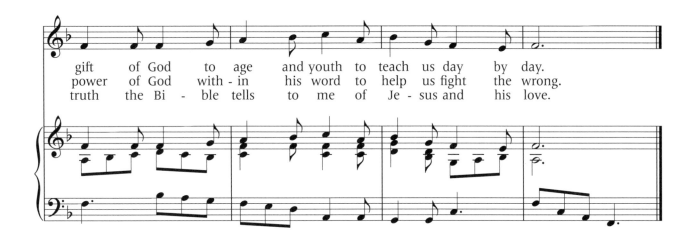

gift of God to age and youth to teach us day by day.
power of God with-in his word to help us fight the wrong.
truth the Bi - ble tells to me of Je - sus and his love.

T HE BIBLE is a shining light,
shining light, shining light,
a lamp to lead us through the night
and guide us on our way.
The Bible is a book of truth,
book of truth, book of truth,
the gift of God to age and youth
to teach us day by day.

2 The Bible is our daily bread,
daily bread, daily bread,
the food by which our souls are fed
to keep us true and strong.
The Bible is the Spirit's sword,
Spirit's sword, Spirit's sword,
the power of God within his word
to help us fight the wrong.

3 The Bible is the living seed,
living seed, living seed,
to grow within us, as we read,
the life of God above.
So open, Lord, my eyes to see,
eyes to see, eyes to see,
the truth the Bible tells to me
of Jesus and his love.

Words: Timothy Dudley-Smith © administered by Oxford University Press in Europe (including UK and Ireland) and
Africa, and by Hope Publishing Company in all other territories (including USA)
Music: William Llewellyn © 2017 Oxford University Press, Great Clarendon Street, Oxford OX2 6DP

17 We are soldiers of the King

MARCH AND SING

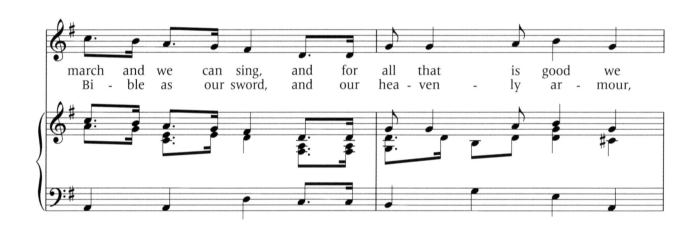

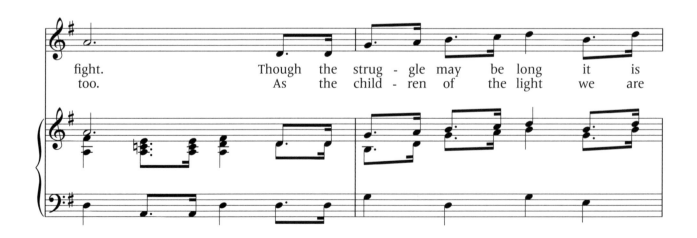

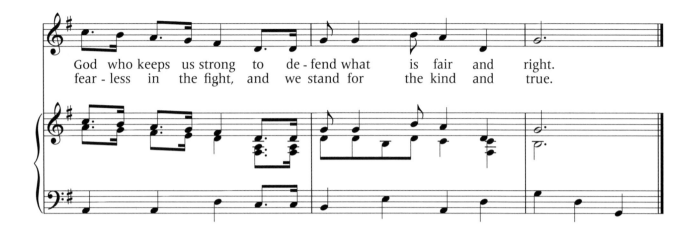

God who keeps us strong to de-fend what is fair and right.
fear-less in the fight, and we stand for the kind and true.

WE ARE SOLDIERS of the King,
we can march and we can sing,
   and for all that is good we fight.
Though the struggle may be long
it is God who keeps us strong
   to defend what is fair and right.

2 We are soldiers of the Lord
with the Bible as our sword,
   and our heavenly armour, too.
As the children of the light
we are fearless in the fight,
   and we stand for the kind and true.

Words: Timothy Dudley-Smith © administered by Oxford University Press in Europe (including UK and Ireland) and
Africa, and by Hope Publishing Company in all other territories (including USA)
Music: William Llewellyn © 2017 Oxford University Press, Great Clarendon Street, Oxford OX2 6DP

18 Tell the world

TELL THE WORLD

Tell the world, tell the world! We have news, we have news, of a

God who is Love, who is swift to for-give, and who sent us his Son as our

Sa - viour and Friend: Hal - le - lu - jah to Je - sus the Son!_

TELL the world,
tell the world!
We have news,
we have news,
  of a God who is Love,
  who is swift to forgive,
and who sent us his Son
as our Saviour and Friend:
  Hallelujah
  to Jesus the Son!

Words: Timothy Dudley-Smith © administered by Oxford University Press in Europe (including UK and Ireland) and
Africa, and by Hope Publishing Company in all other territories (including USA)
Music: William Llewellyn © 2017 Oxford University Press, Great Clarendon Street, Oxford OX2 6DP

19 This wonderful world we live in

CARE FOR THE WORLD

1. This won-der-ful world we live in_____ is
2. All peo-ple on earth are neigh-bours,___ their

not as God meant it to be;_____ he want-ed to see his child-ren_____ all
bro-thers and sis-ters are we;_____ Lord, help us to make our plan-et_____ what

hap - py, heal - thy and free._____ But some of__ world we live in,_____ the
you have meant it to be;_____ to work for a world much fair - er,_____ with

earth, the air and the sea,_____ we have not yet learned to
child - ren hap-py and free,_____ of just-ice and peace and

care for,_____ as God once meant it to be._____
plen - ty,_____ as you have meant it to be._____

THIS WONDERFUL WORLD we live in
is not as God meant it to be;
he wanted to see his children
all happy, healthy and free.
But some of the world we live in,
the earth, the air and the sea,
we have not yet learnt to care for,
as God once meant it to be.

2 All people on earth are neighbours,
their brothers and sisters are we;
Lord, help us to make our planet
what you have meant it to be;
to work for a world much fairer,
with children happy and free,
of justice and peace and plenty,
as you have meant it to be.

Words: Timothy Dudley-Smith © administered by Oxford University Press in Europe (including UK and Ireland) and
Africa, and by Hope Publishing Company in all other territories (including USA)
Music: William Llewellyn © 2017 Oxford University Press, Great Clarendon Street, Oxford OX2 6DP

20 Jesus' friends are one big family

ONE BIG FAMILY

1. Je - sus' friends are one big fam-i-ly, one big fam-i-ly,
2. We are part of one big fam-i-ly, one big fam-i-ly,
3. Jes - sus' friends are one big fam-i-ly, one big fam-i-ly,

one big fam-i-ly! God, who gave us birth,____ calls his child-ren____
one big fam-i-ly, known as Je-sus' friends;____ life is ours as____
one big fam-i-ly! God, who reigns a-bove____ sees us all as____

one big fam-i-ly, all a - cross the earth.__
one big fam-i-ly, life that nev-er ends.__
one big fam-i-ly, child-ren of his love.

One big fam-i-ly!

JESUS' FRIENDS are one big family,
one big family, one big family!
God, who gave us birth,
calls his children one big family
all across the earth.

2 We are part of one big family,
one big family, one big family,
known as Jesus' friends;
life is ours as one big family,
life that never ends.

3 Jesus' friends are one big family,
one big family, one big family!
God who reigns above
sees us all as one big family,
children of his love.

Words: Timothy Dudley-Smith © administered by Oxford University Press in Europe (including UK and Ireland) and
Africa, and by Hope Publishing Company in all other territories (including USA)
Music: William Llewellyn © 2017 Oxford University Press, Great Clarendon Street, Oxford OX2 6DP

1 Our God made the planets

GOD'S CREATION

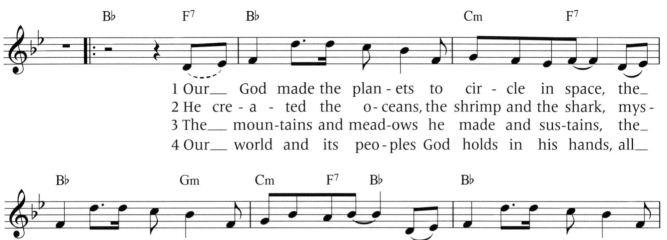

1 Our__ God made the plan-ets to cir-cle in space, the_
2 He cre-a-ted the o-ceans, the shrimp and the shark, mys-
3 The__ moun-tains and mead-ows he made and sus-tains, the_
4 Our__ world and its peo-ples God holds in his hands, all__

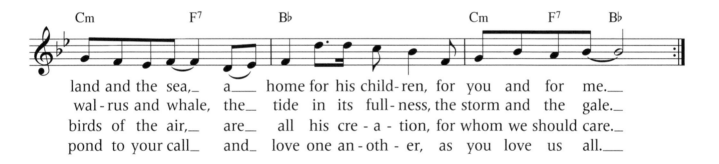

stars in the heav-ens, each star in its place, the_ earth that we live on, the
-te-ri-ous crea-tures who live in the dark, the_ gull and the gan-net, the
sands of the des-ert, the prair-ies and plains; the_ beasts of the jung-le, the
ra-ces and col-ours, all na-tions and lands: may we, as your child-ren, res-

land and the sea,_ a__ home for his child-ren, for you and for me.__
wal-rus and whale, the_ tide in its full-ness, the storm and the gale._
birds of the air,_ are_ all his cre-a-tion, for whom we should care._
pond to your call_ and_ love one an-oth-er, as you love us all.___

Words: Timothy Dudley-Smith © administered by Oxford University Press in Europe (including UK and Ireland) and
Africa, and by Hope Publishing Company in all other territories (including USA)
Music: William Llewellyn © 2017 Oxford University Press, Great Clarendon Street, Oxford OX2 6DP

If your church has a CCLI Music Reproduction Licence, these pages may be photocopied for church use.
Please report usage of these songs in your annual reporting to CCLI.

2 God is Love, God is Love!

KIND AND LOVING

♩. = 96

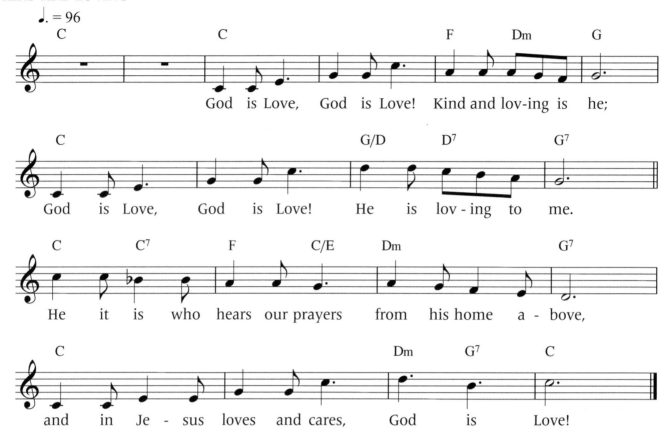

God is Love, God is Love! Kind and lov-ing is he;
God is Love, God is Love! He is lov-ing to me.
He it is who hears our prayers from his home a-bove,
and in Je-sus loves and cares, God is Love!

Words: Timothy Dudley-Smith © administered by Oxford University Press in Europe (including UK and Ireland) and Africa, and by Hope Publishing Company in all other territories (including USA)
Music: William Llewellyn © 2017 Oxford University Press, Great Clarendon Street, Oxford OX2 6DP

If your church has a CCLI Music Reproduction Licence, these pages may be photocopied for church use.
Please report usage of these songs in your annual reporting to CCLI.

3 The Bible tells of Jesus' birth

THE BIBLE TELLS

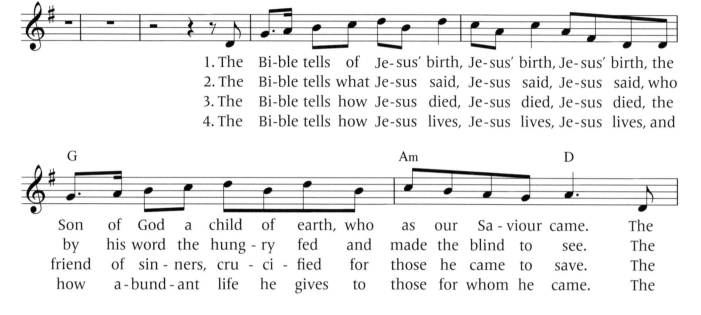

1. The Bi-ble tells of Je-sus' birth, Je-sus' birth, Je-sus' birth, the
2. The Bi-ble tells what Je-sus said, Je-sus said, Je-sus said, who
3. The Bi-ble tells how Je-sus died, Je-sus died, Je-sus died, the
4. The Bi-ble tells how Je-sus lives, Je-sus lives, Je-sus lives, and

Son of God a child of earth, who as our Sa-viour came. The
by his word the hung-ry fed and made the blind to see. The
friend of sin-ners, cru-ci-fied for those he came to save. The
how a-bund-ant life he gives to those for whom he came. The

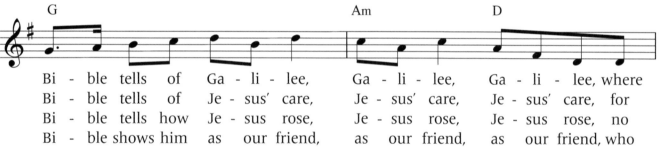

Bi-ble tells of Ga-li-lee, Ga-li-lee, Ga-li-lee, where
Bi-ble tells of Je-sus' care, Je-sus' care, Je-sus' care, for
Bi-ble tells how Je-sus rose, Je-sus rose, Je-sus rose, no
Bi-ble shows him as our friend, as our friend, as our friend, who

Je-sus taught be-side the sea, and healed the sick and lame.
all God's child-ren ev-ery-where, in-clud-ing you and me.
long-er now in death's re-pose but ris-en from the grave!
walks be-side us to the end, and knows us all by name.

Words: Timothy Dudley-Smith © administered by Oxford University Press in Europe (including UK and Ireland) and Africa, and by Hope Publishing Company in all other territories (including USA)
Music: William Llewellyn © 2017 Oxford University Press, Great Clarendon Street, Oxford OX2 6DP

If your church has a CCLI Music Reproduction Licence, these pages may be photocopied for church use.
Please report usage of these songs in your annual reporting to CCLI.

4 Give thanks to Jesus

GIVE THANKS

1. Give thanks to Je-sus, give praise to his Name;

born as our Sa-viour, from heav-en he came; li-ving a-mong us, our

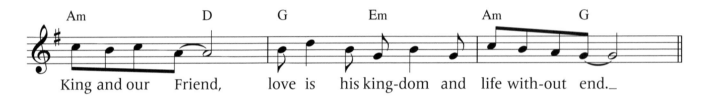

King and our Friend, love is his king-dom and life with-out end._

2. With his Fa-ther he now reigns a-bove; in his king-dom he is King of Love.

To us his chil-dren he shows what to do:____

'Love one an-oth-er, as I have loved you.'___

Words: Timothy Dudley-Smith © administered by Oxford University Press in Europe (including UK and Ireland) and Africa, and by Hope Publishing Company in all other territories (including USA)
Music: William Llewellyn © 2017 Oxford University Press, Great Clarendon Street, Oxford OX2 6DP

If your church has a CCLI Music Reproduction Licence, these pages may be photocopied for church use.
Please report usage of these songs in your annual reporting to CCLI.

5 Jesus taught us to be kind and loving

JESUS TAUGHT US

Words: Timothy Dudley-Smith © administered by Oxford University Press in Europe (including UK and Ireland) and
Africa, and by Hope Publishing Company in all other territories (including USA)
Music: William Llewellyn © 2017 Oxford University Press, Great Clarendon Street, Oxford OX2 6DP

If your church has a CCLI Music Reproduction Licence, these pages may be photocopied for church use.
Please report usage of these songs in your annual reporting to CCLI.

6 Jesus our King

SING TO THE KING

Je-sus our King, Lord and Sa-viour! Je-sus our friend, with us now:__ joy-full-y sing, he is near us, and will hear us sing to the King!__

Words: Timothy Dudley-Smith © administered by Oxford University Press in Europe (including UK and Ireland) and Africa, and by Hope Publishing Company in all other territories (including USA)
Music: William Llewellyn © 2017 Oxford University Press, Great Clarendon Street, Oxford OX2 6DP

If your church has a CCLI Music Reproduction Licence, these pages may be photocopied for church use.

Please report usage of these songs in your annual reporting to CCLI.

7 Spirit of God, be here among us

SPIRIT AMONG US

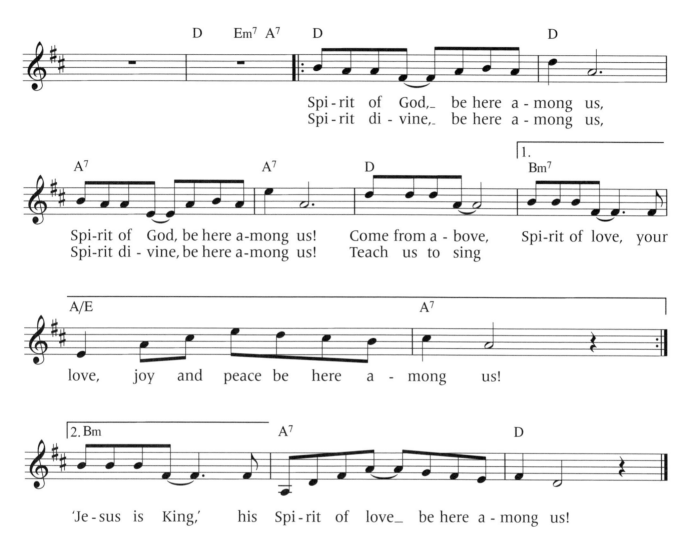

Words: Timothy Dudley-Smith © administered by Oxford University Press in Europe (including UK and Ireland) and Africa, and by Hope Publishing Company in all other territories (including USA)
Music: William Llewellyn © 2017 Oxford University Press, Great Clarendon Street, Oxford OX2 6DP

If your church has a CCLI Music Reproduction Licence, these pages may be photocopied for church use.

Please report usage of these songs in your annual reporting to CCLI.

8 So still, so still!

SO STILL

Rocking gently

1. So still,———— so still!———— the star-light is frost-y and chill; the flocks are a-sleep while shep-herds must keep their watch in the night on the hill:———— there on the hill,———— so still!————
2. Till dawn,———— till dawn!———— there breaks what a won-der-ful morn! With an-gels we sing to wel-come our King; King Je-sus the Sa-viour is born!———— Je-sus is born,———— is born!————
3. Sing praise,———— sing praise!———— a ca-rol of thank-ful-ness raise! God gave in his love his Son from a-bove at Christ-mas, the day of all days,———— day of all days!———— Sing praise!————

Words: Timothy Dudley-Smith © administered by Oxford University Press in Europe (including UK and Ireland) and Africa, and by Hope Publishing Company in all other territories (including USA)
Music: William Llewellyn © 2017 Oxford University Press, Great Clarendon Street, Oxford OX2 6DP

If your church has a CCLI Music Reproduction Licence, these pages may be photocopied for church use.
Please report usage of these songs in your annual reporting to CCLI.

9 When Jesus Christ was all alone

CHRIST TEMPTED

Words: Timothy Dudley-Smith © administered by Oxford University Press in Europe (including UK and Ireland) and Africa, and by Hope Publishing Company in all other territories (including USA)
Music: William Llewellyn © 2017 Oxford University Press, Great Clarendon Street, Oxford OX2 6DP

If your church has a CCLI Music Reproduction Licence, these pages may be photocopied for church use.
Please report usage of these songs in your annual reporting to CCLI.

10 Jesus was riding on a donkey

HOSANNA TO THE KING

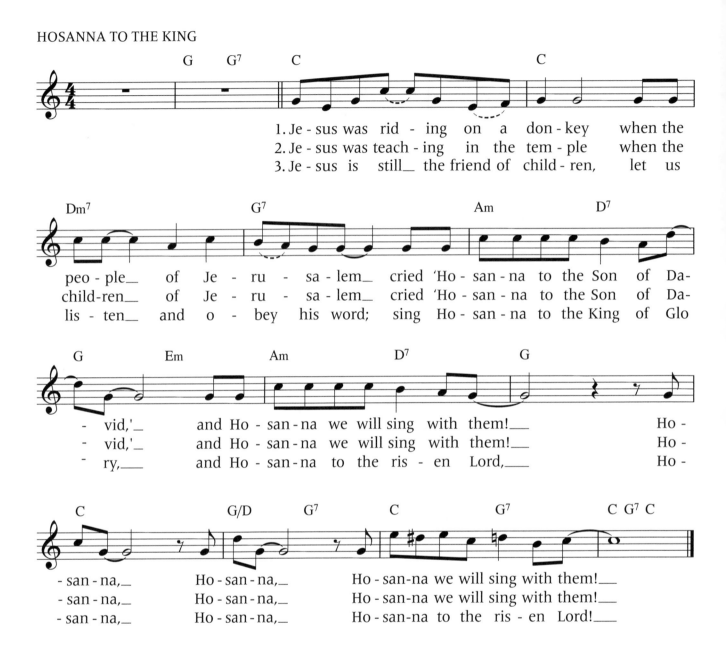

1. Je-sus was rid-ing on a don-key when the peo-ple_ of Je-ru-sa-lem_ cried 'Ho-san-na to the Son of Da-vid,'_ and Ho-san-na we will sing with them!_ Ho-san-na,_ Ho-san-na,_ Ho-san-na we will sing with them!_
2. Je-sus was teach-ing in the tem-ple when the child-ren_ of Je-ru-sa-lem_ cried 'Ho-san-na to the Son of Da-vid,'_ and Ho-san-na we will sing with them!_ Ho-san-na,_ Ho-san-na,_ Ho-san-na we will sing with them!_
3. Je-sus is still_ the friend of child-ren, let us lis-ten_ and o-bey his word; sing Ho-san-na to the King of Glo-ry,___ and Ho-san-na to the ris-en Lord,___ Ho-san-na,_ Ho-san-na,_ Ho-san-na to the ris-en Lord!_

Words: Timothy Dudley-Smith © administered by Oxford University Press in Europe (including UK and Ireland) and Africa, and by Hope Publishing Company in all other territories (including USA)
Music: William Llewellyn © 2017 Oxford University Press, Great Clarendon Street, Oxford OX2 6DP

If your church has a CCLI Music Reproduction Licence, these pages may be photocopied for church use.
Please report usage of these songs in your annual reporting to CCLI.

11 Jesus, once you suffered for me

JESUS SET ME FREE

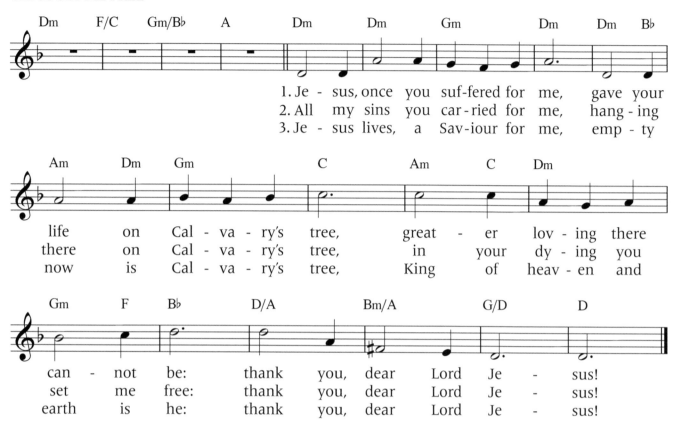

1. Je - sus, once you suf-fered for me, gave your life on Cal - va - ry's tree, great - er lov - ing there can - not be: thank you, dear Lord Je - sus!

2. All my sins you car - ried for me, hang - ing there on Cal - va - ry's tree, in your dy - ing you set me free: thank you, dear Lord Je - sus!

3. Je - sus lives, a Sav-iour for me, emp - ty now is Cal - va - ry's tree, King of heav - en and earth is he: thank you, dear Lord Je - sus!

Words: Timothy Dudley-Smith © administered by Oxford University Press in Europe (including UK and Ireland) and Africa, and by Hope Publishing Company in all other territories (including USA)
Music: William Llewellyn © 2017 Oxford University Press, Great Clarendon Street, Oxford OX2 6DP

If your church has a CCLI Music Reproduction Licence, these pages may be photocopied for church use.
Please report usage of these songs in your annual reporting to CCLI.

12 Jesus risen! The stone rolled away

JESUS RISEN

Je - sus ris - en! The stone rolled a - way!

Come and see where his poor bo - dy lay.__ Je - sus ris - en, in

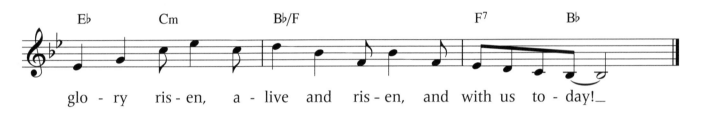

glo - ry ris - en, a - live and ris - en, and with us to - day!__

Words: Timothy Dudley-Smith © administered by Oxford University Press in Europe (including UK and Ireland) and Africa, and by Hope Publishing Company in all other territories (including USA)
Music: William Llewellyn © 2017 Oxford University Press, Great Clarendon Street, Oxford OX2 6DP

If your church has a CCLI Music Reproduction Licence, these pages may be photocopied for church use.
Please report usage of these songs in your annual reporting to CCLI.

13 I am with you always

LOVE ALWAYS

1. I am with you al-ways, al-ways, al-ways, I am with you al-ways, Je-sus gave his word; I am with you al-ways, al-ways, al-ways, I am with you al-ways, Sav-iour, Friend and Lord.

2. I am with you al-ways, al-ways, al-ways, I am with you al-ways, if you are my friend; I am with you al-ways, al-ways, al-ways, I am with you al-ways, to the journ-ey's end.

3. We would love you al-ways, al-ways, al-ways, we would love you al-ways, we will be your friends; we would love you al-ways, al-ways, al-ways, we would love you al-ways till the journ-ey ends!

Words: Timothy Dudley-Smith © administered by Oxford University Press in Europe (including UK and Ireland) and Africa, and by Hope Publishing Company in all other territories (including USA)
Music: William Llewellyn © 2017 Oxford University Press, Great Clarendon Street, Oxford OX2 6DP

If your church has a CCLI Music Reproduction Licence, these pages may be photocopied for church use.
Please report usage of these songs in your annual reporting to CCLI.

14 For the world that we live in

PRAISE FOR THE WORLD

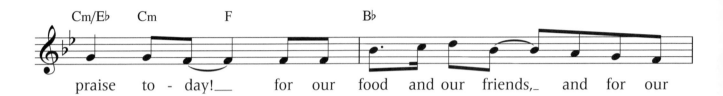

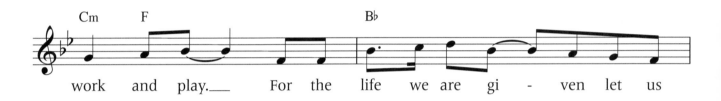

Words: Timothy Dudley-Smith © administered by Oxford University Press in Europe (including UK and Ireland) and
Africa, and by Hope Publishing Company in all other territories (including USA)
Music: William Llewellyn © 2017 Oxford University Press, Great Clarendon Street, Oxford OX2 6DP

If your church has a CCLI Music Reproduction Licence, these pages may be photocopied for church use.
Please report usage of these songs in your annual reporting to CCLI.

15 Lord, we want to learn to pray

PRAISE AND PRAY

1. Lord, we want to learn to pray, read the Bi-ble day by day,
3. Teach us how to praise and pray, read the Bi-ble day by day,

un - der-stand, be - lieve, o - bey, Je - sus our Lord.___
live our lives in Je - sus' way, Je - sus our Lord.___

2. Lord, we want to learn to pray, help us mean the words we say,

live our lives in Je - sus' way, Je - sus our Lord.___

Fa - ther God, at home in heaven, thank you for the

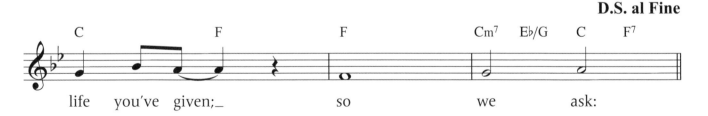

life you've given;___ so we ask:

Words: Timothy Dudley-Smith © administered by Oxford University Press in Europe (including UK and Ireland) and
Africa, and by Hope Publishing Company in all other territories (including USA)
Music: William Llewellyn © 2017 Oxford University Press, Great Clarendon Street, Oxford OX2 6DP

If your church has a CCLI Music Reproduction Licence, these pages may be photocopied for church use.
Please report usage of these songs in your annual reporting to CCLI.

16 The Bible is a shining light

SHINING LIGHT

1. The Bi-ble is a shin-ing light, shin-ing light, shin-ing light, a lamp to lead us through the night and guide us on our way.___ The Bi-ble is a book of truth, book of truth, book of truth, the gift of God to age and youth to teach us day by day.

2. The Bi-ble is our dai-ly bread, dai-ly bread, dai-ly bread, the food by which our souls are fed to keep us true and strong.___ The Bi-ble is the Spi-rit's sword, Spi-rit's sword, Spi-rit's sword, the power of God with-in his word to help us fight the wrong.

3. The Bi-ble is the liv-ing seed, liv-ing seed, liv-ing seed, to grow with-in us, as we read, the life of God a-bove.___ So o-pen, Lord, my eyes to see, eyes to see, eyes to see, the truth the Bi-ble tells to me of Je-sus and his love.

Words: Timothy Dudley-Smith © administered by Oxford University Press in Europe (including UK and Ireland) and Africa, and by Hope Publishing Company in all other territories (including USA)
Music: William Llewellyn © 2017 Oxford University Press, Great Clarendon Street, Oxford OX2 6DP

If your church has a CCLI Music Reproduction Licence, these pages may be photocopied for church use.
Please report usage of these songs in your annual reporting to CCLI.

17 We are soldiers of the King

MARCH AND SING

1. We are sold - iers of the King, we can
2. We are sold - iers of the Lord with the

march and we can sing, and for all that is good we
Bi - ble as our sword, and our hea - ven - ly ar - mour,

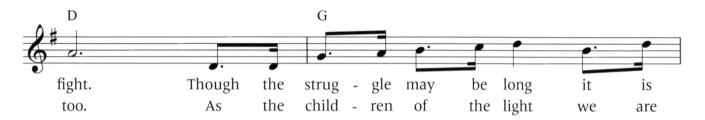

fight. Though the strug - gle may be long it is
too. As the child - ren of the light we are

God who keeps us strong to de - fend what is fair and right.
fear - less in the fight, and we stand for the kind and true.

Words: Timothy Dudley-Smith © administered by Oxford University Press in Europe (including UK and Ireland) and Africa, and by Hope Publishing Company in all other territories (including USA)
Music: William Llewellyn © 2017 Oxford University Press, Great Clarendon Street, Oxford OX2 6DP

If your church has a CCLI Music Reproduction Licence, these pages may be photocopied for church use.
Please report usage of these songs in your annual reporting to CCLI.

18 Tell the world

TELL THE WORLD

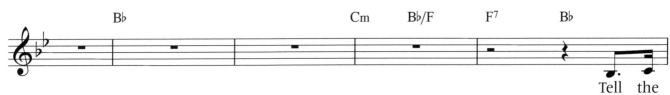

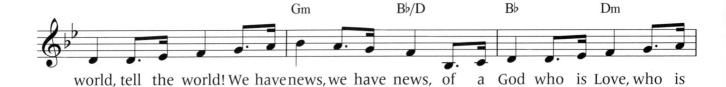

world, tell the world! We have news, we have news, of a God who is Love, who is

swift to for-give, and who sent us his Son as our Sa - viour and Friend:

Hal - le - lu - jah to Je - sus the Son!__

Words: Timothy Dudley-Smith © administered by Oxford University Press in Europe (including UK and Ireland) and Africa, and by Hope Publishing Company in all other territories (including USA)
Music: William Llewellyn © 2017 Oxford University Press, Great Clarendon Street, Oxford OX2 6DP

If your church has a CCLI Music Reproduction Licence, these pages may be photocopied for church use.
Please report usage of these songs in your annual reporting to CCLI.

19 This wonderful world we live in

CARE FOR THE WORLD

Words: Timothy Dudley-Smith © administered by Oxford University Press in Europe (including UK and Ireland) and Africa, and by Hope Publishing Company in all other territories (including USA)
Music: William Llewellyn © 2017 Oxford University Press, Great Clarendon Street, Oxford OX2 6DP

If your church has a CCLI Music Reproduction Licence, these pages may be photocopied for church use.
Please report usage of these songs in your annual reporting to CCLI.

20 Jesus' friends are one big family

ONE BIG FAMILY

Words: Timothy Dudley-Smith © administered by Oxford University Press in Europe (including UK and Ireland) and Africa, and by Hope Publishing Company in all other territories (including USA)
Music: William Llewellyn © 2017 Oxford University Press, Great Clarendon Street, Oxford OX2 6DP

If your church has a CCLI Music Reproduction Licence, these pages may be photocopied for church use.
Please report usage of these songs in your annual reporting to CCLI.